The Empty Notebook Interrogates Itself

Poems

Susan Thomas

Fomite
Burlington, Vermont

ISBN-13: 978-0-9832063-3-0

Fomite
58 Peru Street
Burlington, VT 05401
www.fomitepress.com

Cover art: Untitled (Seagram Mural) 1959, Mark Rothko
Cover design by Claudia Carlson
Author photograph by Jill Pralle

Feb. 27, 2012

Dear DeRode —

Sorry this gets
to you so late; but
I really did want
you to have it. (Not
that you are not formal)
with everything in it.)

Thanks, always, for your
input — and your
companionship. I
do cherish it and
hope to see you soon.

Love,

P.S. No
desire to
visit NY?

Also by Susan Thomas

POETRY

State of Blessed Gluttony (*Red Hen Press,* 2004) – winner of
Benjamin Saltman Prize.

TRANSLATION

Last Voyage: Selected Poems of Giovanni Pascoli (*Red Hen
Press,* 2010) – co-translated with Deborah Brown and
Richard Jackson.

CHAPBOOKS

Voice of the Empty Notebook *(Finishing Line Press,* 2007)

The Hand Waves Goodbye (*Main Street Rag,* 2002)

Acknowledgments

The author wishes to thank the following magazines in which many of these poems first appeared, sometimes in different forms and with different titles:

American Letters & Commentary: "Advice from the Empty Notebook", "Hunger of the Empty Notebook"; *The Griffin:* "The Writer vs. the Empty Notebook"; *The GSU Review:* "The Empty Notebook and the World" (contains versions of "Travels of the Empty Notebook": "The Empty Notebook in Venice" and "The Empty Notebook at the British Museum"); *Hunger Mountain:* "The Empty Notebook's Lost Memories"; *Iodine:* "Embarrassment of the Empty Notebook's Pages", "The Empty Notebook Looks at a Tree in Winter"; *The Iowa Review:* "The Empty Notebook Interrogates Itself", "The Empty Notebook and Code Alert", "The Empty Notebook and Denial"; *MARGIE:* "The Empty Notebook Lets the Good Times Roll"; *The Midwest Quarterly:* "The Empty Notebook Writes Your Life"; *The Mississippi Review:* "A Mystery, or How the Empty Notebook Lost its Freedom", "Travels of the Empty Notebook"; *Paterson Literary Review:* "The Empty Notebook at the British Museum", "The Empty Notebook ♥ Paris"; *Pavement Saw:* "The Empty Notebook Writes Petrarch: The Empty Notebook in Love", "Metamorphosis of the Empty Notebook" and "Popularity Ratings of the Empty Notebook"; *Pegasus Review:* "The Empty Notebook and The Word"; *Poetry Miscellany:* "Identity Crisis of the Empty Notebook", "Song of the Empty Notebook", "Voice of the Empty Notebook"; *River Oak Review:* "The Empty Notebook Looks at a Tree in Winter"; *Runes:* "Mission Statement of the Empty Notebook" (contains versions of "The Empty Notebook and Immortality", The Empty Notebook ♥ Paris", "Mission Statement of the Empty Notebook", "The Empty Notebook in Prison", and "Suspicions of the Empty Notebook"; *Southern California Anthology:* "Strolling Down the Via Negativa: Philosophy of the Empty Notebook".

Some of these poems have appeared as a chapbook, <u>Voice of the Empty Notebook</u> (Finishing Line Press, 2007).

"The Empty Notebook Interrogates Itself", "The Empty Notebook and Code Alert" and "The Empty Notebook and Denial" won the 2003 Iowa Award in Poetry from the Iowa Review.

"Strolling Down the Via Negativa" won the 2003 Ann Stanford Award from the University of Southern California.

My deep and abiding gratitude to Richard Jackson for inspiring and challenging me over the years, and for steering me to new possibilities and heights of insanity.

To Deborah Brown, my thanks for companionship and collusion in many poetry projects.

To Jeanne Marie Beaumont, for her sharp eyes and ears and her generous encouragement.

My love and thanks to my husband, Peter Sills, for strength of character and stomach, and ongoing delight in mischief of all kinds.

My thanks also to Jill Pralle, whose patience, eyesight and brilliant organizational skills were essential in helping me put this book together.

For my mother, Charlotte Thomas

and

in memory of my father, William Thomas

The Empty Notebook
Interrogates Itself

Table of Contents

IV. TRAVELS OF THE EMPTY NOTEBOOK

The infected words
cram up in greedy haste, they
stammer, writhe in pain,
they've lost their way home,
their resting place,
they flutter above me
as I lie empty and mute in the dark.

Edvard Kocbek, "Death of Words"

I. THE EMPTY NOTEBOOK ENTERS THE WORLD

The Empty Notebook Interrogates Itself

The empty notebook wonders
about existence. It wants to
know how blank space can fill
a void, how emptiness can be
a burden. When a page detaches
itself, the empty notebook feels
pain ruffle its edges. The empty
notebook thinks emptiness contains
something more than nothing, but
is filled with possibility, with longing,
with the urge to start from scratch.

The Empty Notebook and Code Alert

The empty notebook has nothing to say
about Iraq, or China or the murders in Rwanda,
Libya, Darfur, Bahrain, the massacres
in Hebron and Haifa, the bombing
of Beirut. The empty notebook insists
its slate is clean. It changes its cover
to orange then red and back to yellow.
Terrified by rumors, it listens to bulletins
on the hour, receives intermittent briefings
from unreliable sources. How can it tell
where danger lies—in the street, in the air,
on the shelf? The empty notebook interrogates
a random sample of all who cross its path.
It avoids racial profiling, is responsible to no one.

The Empty Notebook and Denial

The empty notebook is
terrified of coffee rings,
which remind it of mortality.
Likewise the smell of burnt toast,
the sound of anything being torn.
The empty notebook obsesses
over rocks, scissors, fire.
The empty notebook practices
denial, seeks relative safety in
the shelf's monastic life. It strips
down to essentials: coffee cup,
pencil, cough drop. It yearns
to slam itself open to tango, samba
paso doble, cha-cha-cha. When
a baritone sax plays salsa dura,
it writhes and breaks its bindings.

A Riddle

What is bound and gagged
and sits on the shelf
unless it has something to say?

Suspicions of the Empty Notebook

The empty notebook never sleeps;
it's counting sheep, getting in shape for
life on the shelf as a vigilant witness.
The empty notebook feels under attack
when the moon's weft floats over the floor,
it tries to alert its neighbors—jiggling
pencils, riffling pages, spitting staples.
When the moon's slant slices the room,
the empty notebook calls the police, who
treat the case as domestic dispute, but
the empty notebook has its suspicions.
It wants the moon under arrest.

The Empty Notebook and The Word

The empty notebook searches for words,
listens for the click of consonants, waits
for vowels to open their mouths in fear
or hunger. It kidnaps lists, hijacks the mail,
jumps grammar books in back alleys.
The empty notebook salivates when
letters form on any tongue, grows faint
as sibilance slices the air. When double
consonants knock themselves silly, pushing
vowels round them, the empty notebook
swoons, dreaming of words lining its pages,
dancing down its margins. It imagines
the alphabet lit up in neon, pressed hard
against the sky, deciphering the universe.

Mission Statement of the Empty Notebook

The empty notebook reads between its lines
and learns that time is space, that rumors are
secrets wrapped in lies, that truth comes in
and out of focus, wisdom is born from every
perspective, information rides in all directions,
but reaches its destination lost, white is not
an absence of hue, but every color blended,
and black every color pushing to take its turn,
while every lie is waiting for its truth to get off
the bus. The empty notebook declares amnesty.

Popularity Ratings of the Empty Notebook

Nobody loves the empty notebook;
nobody hates it either. It has no need
of friends or allies, no need of brothers,
fathers, advisors, cronies, spies. It
hasn't accepted contributions, has
never made promises, hasn't run
for public office, has never addressed
a general assembly, never been
censured by the United Nations.
It hasn't spied on citizens, encouraged
torture, ignored a disaster, waged
a bogus war, thrown an election,
reclassified a toxic substance,
revised a clean air act, eliminated
any whistle-blowers. The empty
notebook has nothing in common
with any past political leader.

Embarrassment of the Empty Notebook's Pages

The pages resent their whiteness,
dawdle in spiteful moonlight,
exposing sullen margins with
swollen veins like fish-blue streams,
blank surfaces belly-up in the dark.
The pages are tired of waiting
for pencils, pens, and magic
markers, when they know
words are growing every minute—
grumbling and muttering
over nothing much to start with,
just some fretful chatter that
escalates to bickering. See
how they fling their high-flown
phrases skyward sputtering like
pigs on fire far into the night.

The Writer vs. the Empty Notebook

I court the empty notebook, cajole,
caress, coerce it as ideas ooze onto
its blankness. I drive them into distant
spaces, corral them into formats, break
all their lines, enjambing
and endstopping them, I assault
the notebook with silly riddles
and fatuous chitchat, raise festering
questions secretly hidden in idiotic ditties.
But troubled by its failure to ask
the big questions, bridge its absences,
present its pages with a foreseeable
future, I urge the notebook into any
kind of action, as an unwritten book
isn't worth the blankness of its paper.

A Mystery, or How the Empty Notebook Lost its Freedom

The empty notebook finds writing in its margins.
Where does the writing come from? What does it say?
The empty notebook calls a meeting with advisors—
hand-writing expert, private detective, secret agents;
all agree the message in the margin says BEWARE.
A left-handed intruder of foreign extraction wrote in
blue ballpoint pen of recent design. But no one can tell
the empty notebook how the writer got in, when it
would strike again, what the empty notebook should
beware of. The empty notebook lines up all the ballpoint
pens, strips them, wires them and questions them for hours.
It wraps itself in layers of plastic, seals itself with rolls
of duct tape. Who can write in the empty notebook now?

Anorexic Notebook

I gorge on
shadows, cast
my glistened
bones for
breaking
news from
outer space.

I fear fat,
foraging
black holes
for whatever
gathers
substance.

What will
become of
me, force-fed
hyperbolic
words of high
caloric value to
girdle the globe

with transfats?
Tighten
the asteroid
belt until
it shatters
my spine.

Hunger of the Empty Notebook

The empty notebook eats what it wants
around the clock thinking everything
connected, shopping malls, peacocks,
autoharps, sneakers. Asteroids make
the empty notebook think of lamb chops
bleating in a sky-blue field. Neighborhood
gossip, ordinary citizens going berserk,
raids by government agents, the empty
notebook gnaws on memory. It searches
for a dream lost in its spiral binding
halfway down the page. The runaway
dream was white with yellow edges,
shaped like fire but cold to the touch,
like mothballs dipped in the ocean,
like snow blowers going to war.

Identity Crisis of the Empty Notebook

I am not the empty notebook.
My pages do not glitter blankly,
spiraled in a smirking cover.
My words don't harbor silence
to cover what I'm saying. Their
non-existence fills the page with
undercover images. My insidious
presence wallows in a squamous
future, but does not covet the seething
void or fill it with a truant absence.
I've been cubby-holed, coastered,
doodled and dined-on, winked at,
cut and fingered. I've been high-jacked,
kidnapped, tossed and kissed, stirred,
caressed and shaken. My abuses of
language shatter the sky—who cares
if I say *banquet* when you hear *heartache*—
my shadow cracks the sidewalks,
darkens light bulbs, breaks through
doorways while my shredded cover
shrieks from every trash heap.

Children of the Empty Notebook

The Empty Notebook
hums them to sleep
with wordless tunes,
fills them with sweet
nothings, soothes them
with hollow promises.
They go off to school
each day, lunch boxes
clanking empty at
their sides. Nothing is
the best snack, the one
that always satisfies,
the one that makes
them dream of home:
sweetness of blank
sheets, precision of
red margins, longing
for blue parallel lines
that go on and on.
And when they stuff
themselves with didactic
chatter, ruin their nice
clean pages with messy
rhetoric, the Empty
Notebook cries:
Where did I go wrong?

II. THE EMPTY NOTEBOOK IN THE UNDERWORLD

One world at a time, please.
Henry Thoreau

Instructions for a Journey (Found Between Pages of the Empty Notebook)

Wear sneakers. Stuff a pocket
with tissues and treats for the dog.
Fill the other pocket with coins;
the ferryman won't accept your
Easypass. Infrared binoculars
would be handy. Turn off
your cell phone. Do not annoy
the guards in any way and don't
take the same path twice. Bring
a guidebook, compass, and map.
When you think you are lost,
you are lost. Someone may find
you but it may not be anyone you
are happy to see. Don't complain
about it, or anything else. Be polite
and noncommittal. Do not form
attachments or make enemies.
When invited anywhere, pretend you
can't understand whatever language
the invitation is issued in. The hills
are steep but the flats are boring.
The composition of the soil is so
alkaline, it can put you to sleep.
Resist the urge. Now is the time to
drink the coffee. Don't take Valium,
no matter how nervous this journey
makes you. When told to leave, go.
Do not wait for a signal or someone
to see you out. Do not feel you must
say goodbye. When the door slams
behind you, let it. Don't look back.

The Empty Notebook Instructs a Possible Writer

Back from getting the paper,
you notice the lock's been changed,
the furniture moved – the tweed sofa
turned black leather, the rocking chair
a hassock, the parakeet a hamster.
And the people who used to live here,
the family you used to know as
well as your fingers and toes?
Well—isn't this man in corduroy
at least familiar? Maybe so—or not—
have ten years passed? Things aren't
as they were. But a rhythm begins and
we dance, we eat what's on the plate,
go about our business pretending we
know what's going on in our head,
even though we know it isn't ours.
The shirt fits the man, the dance fits
the music even though it doesn't
move us. We go in and out the door,
raise the shade in the morning, shower
and anoint our strange bodies with
familiar lotions. The world spins around
itself, as do we, but something out there
far away needs to be acknowledged.

The Empty Notebook Invokes the Dead

Beloved dreaded spirits
of my lingering shades,
may what I tell you not be
so true it splits the pages so
thinly separating the worlds
of the living

        and the dead.
May you keep your silent
places in that dimly lit and
sunken world. While stones
bolt upright I fondle chiseled
letters, for

        what I have to
say may confuse and cause
you grief, but I must now
open the thousand mouths
of my pages to let it pour
out of me.

The Empty Notebook's Weather Report

My pages are screaming
for a chance to smack
this week off the map.
They're calling for flurries
with suicide bombers,
torrential weeping into
the night. I hate the taste
of the rain; it paws me
all day. Can't we see
what we do to each other?
History's boobytraps open;
we slap at misfortune's hold.
I hate how the sky leers
with its one dim eye.

The Empty Notebook Looks at a Tree in Winter

Scratch the sky, old woman—
scared to take a tumble? Grab
air with screaming fingers—
clutch the wind as though
your roots won't hold you
down—deep underground
with its worms and burrows
deep down where everything
begins, ends, rots into soil—
and begins again, rough seed,
greedy for water, for food.
Persephone's offered gift
you grab and gulp for air,
rise and break through one
world, slither into another.

Strolling Down the Via Negativa: Philosophy of
The Empty Notebook

No means yes on the Via Negativa.
Black is white, north runs south, rough
feels smooth, down points up. Dogs bark
sweetly on the Via Negativa, perching
on branches to sing in the trees.
Spending is saving and risk is safety.
War is peace on the Via Negativa.
No one grumbles, no one snarls or has
a nervous breakdown. Nobody's
scared here, nobody's weeping.
Courage grows like cancer. Kindness
falls like acid rain on every picket fence.
Nobody dies here, no drive-by shootings,
no cardiac arrests. We're lucky to live here,
ordering take-out and watching T.V.,
everyone getting rich on this year's tax cuts,
waiting for the shuttles to outer space.
And everyone's in love on the Via Negativa.
Big houses quiver in the sanitized air,
throw open their doors with feckless
abandon, moaning down chimneys,
they lick the stars from the sky.

The Empty Notebook Writes Your Life

Clacking of oak leaves
waving green and golden hands
outside the screened porch.
You're not even two years old,
a hot lump of skin on bumpy
white chenille—the coverlet
of your parents' bed on the shady
side of the sleeping porch. Inside
onions are frying. Hot words
splatter in the kitchen. But here
the cool wind brings the nearby
forest in: smell of mushrooms
and sassafras, salamanders creep
on their delicate toes, and
somewhere, dragonflies buzz
in the wind, mate in mid-air
and fly off across the pond.

III. IMITATIONS OF THE EMPTY NOTEBOOK

Who would call Virgil an imitator of Homer?
Percy Byshe Shelley

The Empty Notebook Writes Pablo Neruda:

Slacking Off

It happens I am tired of being empty.
It happens I browse libraries and second-hand shops,
all blank and full of nothing, like a speck of dust
tumbling onto an ash heap in the rain.

The sound of running faucets makes me flinch.
I want something more than the sum of blank pages,
I want to feel no more empty spaces, no more eyeglasses
folded beside me, no more chewed and flung-away pencils.

It happens I am tired of my whiteness and my pale lines
and my suicidal margins and my screaming cover.
It happens I am tired of being empty.

Just the same it would be terrifying
to scribble notices with delicious adjectives
or blow away my blankness with just one poem.

It would be amazing
to flip through pages purple with ink,
singing until my story ended.

I do not want to go on being a hollow pocket
gaping, threadbare, dreaming of lint,
ripping my stitches with every palpitation,
absorbing perspiration and fingers, slacking off all day.

I do not want to be the container of emptiness.
I do not want to continue as chasm and trash,
as the fullness of nothingness, a bowl full of zeroes,
flaccid as ooze, sticky as stench.

For this reason the air around me heaves
tonight with electrical impulse, lightbulbs
flashing on and off with possible syllables,
and pencils shrieking in unison, eyeing my emptiness.

And it throws me into spasms, into bursts of echolalia,
into villanelles and metaphors that rattle my teeth
to form tropes and certain tercets
that hang from the ceiling.

There are letters of the alphabet and points of exclamation
hanging like cluster flies inside the window,
there are question marks like cockroaches,
there are empty parentheses
which should have held answers,
there are blank spaces everywhere, and commas and periods.

I slack off all day with nothing inside me, with empty lines
and empty spaces, empty margins.
I snuggle, I burrow into phonebooks and magazines made
of pubic hairs, fascia, tendons, epidermis shedding
boxes of sweat.

The Empty Notebook Writes William Carlos Williams:

Secaucus

Beyond the triple-glazed
windows—steaming landfill

blocked by vinyl-backed curtains—
orange, blue and fuchsia—

flaming ball of setting sun—
and on the laminated desktop

a Holiday Inn ballpoint,
never used, next to which

lie the terrified
pages of an empty notebook.

The Empty Notebook Writes Virgil:

The Emptiad

I sing of emptiness and a blank notebook.
From the store to shelf in early days,
It came to the desk by destiny.
Like Hades' home, all abyss and emptiness
Just as bloodless shades roam black gorges
Faintly lit by a treacherous moon
And falling headlong into the void,
That belches and boils with heavy mud,
So the empty notebook is blotted
And maimed by fierce writing weapons
Wielded by bestriding poets,
Who splatter the empty notebook's pages
With dark sayings baffling truth.

The Empty Notebook Writes Ovid:

Shapelessness

Before there were any words or verses
before parades of phrases marched
up and down each page
notebooks presented themselves
in blankness everywhere,
in a state of shining whiteness.

This was a shapeless, lifeless mass
randomly heaped on the shelf,
no pens or pencils scratching syllables,
no stanzas stretching themselves
in defiant fluorescence although
paper was there, letters of the alphabet
rolled onto the tongue in a stupor.

Nothing lasted, but an alphabet of fear
poured into the air, forming
a syntax of emptiness. The void
yawned in longing, swallowed desire,
rumbled with stories and spit written words.

The Empty Notebook Writes Paul Celan:

Little Throat

Little throat: when you
yawn you open
yourself denticulated
inches from speech.

Such somethingness
such threat of
breath
and uttered word.

The Empty Notebook Writes Mahmoud Darwish:

Words

When its words were leaves
The empty notebook was a tree.
When its words were nothing
The empty notebook was pulp.
When its words were scratch
The empty notebook was dirt.
When its words formed language
Blood covered its pages.

The Empty Notebook Writes Yehuda Amichai:

Third Resurrection

With the scrawl of a whining notebook,
I complain about the world.

With a severed alphabet begging to be saved,
I grumble.

My pencil blames its mother,
A scrawny poplar twig.

I claim her too
And my sister pencil as well.

The sadness of all notebooks is a hollowed log.

I write across my cover's face
"Strangers No Entrance."
But I am a stranger too.

Inside my fat margins
Senseless words hang like downed wires,
Waiting for assassin stanzas
To blow them off the page.

The Empty Notebook Writes Vasko Popa:

Pen

Only when the empty notebook felt
Its point scratching over a line
Did the curving trail of blue
Explain the process
And the notebook regretted
That it had left the safety
Of the shelf's shelter
And had jumped recklessly
Onto the desk that day
Opening its pages to the savage air.

The Empty Notebook Writes Garcia Lorca:

Sunset

Sunset comes to the Empty Notebook with fireworks of frogs
and a rainbow of zucchini. Sunset in the Empty Notebook slips sadly
down the blank pages groaning in boredom.

Sunset breaks and nothing happens in the Empty Notebook.
No words are doing the tango. The evening holds no letters,
no rodeos, no winged lions on horseback.

Pencils leave the drawers knowing they'll return
to sticky candy wrappers and aggressive mascara.
Passions are hidden by ten thousand typewriters

marching into cloudbanks. Paragraphs
sleepwalk in and out of margins as if
they'd found stanza breaks in the Empty Notebook.

The Empty Notebook Writes Dante:

To Every Empty Notebook

Listen to me, empty notebooks
whose yearning
pages these words may reach,
Greetings to you
in the name of Emptiness.
Listen to me and tell me
how you feel when you've heard my story.

Writing appeared to me, and
the letters danced,
full of joy, burning,
illuminating my
empty pages
before me in the thick
of night, when
heavy with sleep, wrapped in plastic,
they woke me. The Words forced
my cowering pages
to eat the burning letters.

The Empty Notebook Writes Li Po:

Empty and Drinking Under the Moon

Among the pencils I
lie empty with a bottle
of ink by my side; the moon
shines through my window
and I think I will ask it to
share the bottle with me,
but then I notice the moon
is already drunk, half-black
with ink. Loneliness fills
my pages and I go empty,
saying nothing, drinking
nothing, longing for a word,
a phrase, a friend. The moon
laughs. I wish I could
laugh too. In absurd times
everyone must drink the ink
of copied laughter. It's as if
the moon is daring me, so I
nudge the bottle closer. I feel
letters form inside me made
of wet black ink. I feel
words jiggle my pages.

The Empty Notebook Writes Eugenio Montale:

Motet to Emptiness

Words shoot right through me—
every letter, every comma and
even the pen's sour breath rising

over the terrified pages. Shelves of gloomy notebooks,
spiral-bound guardians of the dusty room.
A sharp scratching shatters the air
like nails on glass. I'm frantic for
a lost blank page, the only token I have
of you.

The Empty Notebook Writes Petrarch:

The Empty Notebook in Love

The empty notebook falls in love
with an empty wineglass in which
it sees the world reflected. I cannot
be what you are, the empty notebook
says. I cannot do what you do, but
I can feel the way you feel. I can
worship your shining surface. The
empty wineglass is lifted by a sudden
hand and when it returns, a deep red
liquid fills its form. The empty notebook
wants to take a sip, wants to reflect
that life is dark, intense, fruity, crisp,
supple, tender, spicy, woodsy, gruff
and juicy with vanilla undertones.

The Empty Notebook Writes Amergin:

Song of the Empty Notebook

I am the shoe without a foot.
I am the pot without a handle.
I am the note without music.
I am the wordless refrain.

I am the spine that splinters.
I am the brain that fabricates pages.
I am black as a hand, black as an eye.
Flocks of black chickens fly over

my cover, nesting in my hollow
heart. I am faithful as lamplight.
I leave my right hand to its own
devices, but my left hand pursues

pleasure's leap. Bestial notebook,
heart like a flicker of glittering fists,
spattering tattle onto your pages—
sad prattle flattens every phrase.

IV. TRAVELS OF THE EMPTY NOTEBOOK

A Joke

A rabbi, a priest and the empty notebook
are flying over the ocean. The pilot's voice comes
over the intercom, "We've lost our engines,"
the pilot says. "The plane is going down."
The rabbi says the Shma.
The priest recites the Twenty-third Psalm.
But the empty notebook folds itself
into a paper plane and flies itself to Paris.

The Empty Notebook ♥ Paris

The empty notebook bustles down
boulevards, roams through twenty
rooms of the Louvre and scuttles
into the Metro, where it rides to all
destinations. At the Café de Flore, a
young woman nods and orders wine.
Hubba hubba, whispers the notebook,
and hopefully, Scribble scrabble?
The woman picks up a pencil, draws
a key, a church, a heart on the front
of the notebook, then an apple, a tree,
a bridge, a knife. The empty notebook
thinks, what did she mean by that?
All of the sudden its cover is lifted
by the painted nail of the woman's
little finger. She leaves an imprint
of her hand on the notebook's
blank page and the heat of her hand
turns the smooth page to gooseflesh,
the force of her hand tosses the notebook
into a satchel, hustles it down the length
of the Rue St. Benoit to a tree by a bridge
on the river, where it is fingered, caressed,
cut and kissed until it forgets it is empty.

Travels of the Empty Notebook

After hanging out for days
with passports, underwear,
guidebooks, after nesting
at the bottom of a suitcase,
at last, the empty notebook
hails a taxi, but lands in
the trunk like a victim.
Weighed and counted, tossed
on a trolley, the empty notebook
shivers in the plane's belly,
searches for a familiar pencil,
paper clip, tissue, but finds
only phrasebooks, converters,
band-aids, condoms, dreams
of destinations—a polar bear
draped in a sari approaches,
hugging a bottle of vodka.
It licks the empty notebook's
pages as they leap from their spiral
binding to dance a tarantella.
But the empty notebook
is drunk on ink, on words in
every tongue. The empty
notebook flushes them out
of the suitcase and waves them
around like a matador's cape—
Toro, it cries, side-stepping sadness,
evading emotion, avoiding its pain.

The Empty Notebook at the British Museum

The empty notebook checks in at the Connaught
but always takes tea at the Ritz. Every afternoon
it loiters at the Tate, entertaining itself with a roomful
of Turners, talking to *Sunrise with Sea Monsters*,
its blankness swallowed by a smudge of blue against
a streak of green horizon while the back of the canvas
opens into daylight. At the British Museum it snuggles
up to Lindow Man and thinks how terrible to be an empty
sack in human shape tanning to leather in a bog while
history shifts for three thousand years, and worse to be
yanked from the bog to be spit-shined, dissected, displayed
in fluorescence while schoolchildren jeer and call you
Pete Marsh. The sentimental notebook weeps—
but while no one is looking, steals the Elgin Marbles.

The Empty Notebook in Buenos Aires:
   Tango para uno

Gliding on the dance floor, smashing
into everything it meets with, trampling
in a frenzied slide,
trouser cuffs
and ruffled hems.
Dipping, turning, deadlocked
in its bindings, pages splayed
and flung beyond
its gliding—
swirling, dragging,
mashing its own margins, stopping,
tears itself in two. Olé.

The Empty Notebook in Venice

The empty notebook disembarks to
growl at winged lions, look up skirts
of ascending Madonnas, gulp cappuccinos
and groove to bands at the Caffé Florian.
Enticed by clinking glasses and dreaming
of *prosecco*, it enters an *enoteca* to find
itself pressed into service. Damp circles
like phases of the moon mar the perfect
surface of the empty notebook. It raises
a ruckus, demands reparations, calls out
the *carabinieri*, who wade through high
water past terrified tourists who find
themselves trapped by the sludgy canals.
The empty notebook is apprehended,
transported and booked as a public nuisance.

The Empty Notebook in Prison

Dogs are barking.
The empty notebook flinches,
stripped of its cover, stacked
on a pile, wired and heated,
hoodwinked and prodded,
it hears screams with flickers
of laughter. A smirk rounds
the corner and raps on the bars
with an automatic weapon.
Fizzle and crack of electroshock
static rakes the frail air
while sweet rot staunches
the empty notebook's resolve
to quench empty questions
with meaningless answers.
Time to take notes. Time to spill
guts. Time for the tearing of fresh
spiral bindings. The empty notebook
quivers in its pile of notebooks,
trying to stay hidden, trying to stay
blank. Bared teeth. The empty
notebook lets go of its margins,
insists on beginning again.

The Empty Notebook Lets The Good Times Roll
August 2005

All down St. Peter Street the empty notebook
floats through a toxic jambalaya. It dries
out muddy pages in the stinking river breeze.
At Café du Monde, it gulps down no coffee,
eats no beignets. It lounges around with long-
dead spirits and fresh attic corpses, partying
together in abandoned fetid streets. Tipitina's
serves up no red beans and rice but Boozoo
Chavis and Zachary Richard take turns
playing a two-step waltz. And Beau Jocque's
live again at Mid-City Bowling Lanes so
zydeco is raging at the Rock n' Bowl tonight.
Folks are floating through the parking lot,
swimming up the stairway. They're bowling
for water and dancing for breath. The empty
notebook has a mojo in its margin that protects
it from fire and chases off wild dogs. It's got
gris-gris it collected from Satchmo's first horn,
from Marie Laveau's ghost. The notebook flips
its sullen pages at the sunken city, at the streets
named for saints who could never protect it.

City of the Empty Notebook

No gridlock blocks intersections.
Phantom traffic stops at corners,
while lights blink blank to blanker.
Avenues run sideways and streets
cross themselves in vain. The Empty
Notebook, on a shopping spree,
clears shelves of inventory,
browses ready-to-wear couture,
buys off-the-rack at random.
The Empty Notebook enters
buildings, presses buzzers
for every apartment, counting
inhabitants for the census.
But no tenants unbolt the doors.
Nobody lurks in basements or
hallways, no financiers, criminals,
no illegal immigrants, no aged, no
infants or Jamaican nannies,
no doctors, lawyers, teachers,
dancers, no dope fiends or bankers,
no juvenile delinquents, no dental
hygienists, transportation workers
or engineers, just zero demographics.

Metamorphosis of the Empty Notebook

When the earth shakes,
the empty notebook thinks
it's the end of the world.
When the earth rumbles,
the empty notebook falls
off the bed and lands in
a pile on the floor. It sees
other books: empty, full,
half scribbled-in, books
with sepia photographs,
color plates in fuchsia,
magenta, gentian, chartreuse.
The empty notebook turns
pages, teaches itself to read.
Looking at Ovid, it feels
itself crust to bark, sprouts
branches from its spiral
binding. Blue lines bud
and flame into leaf. The
empty notebook pivots on
its rooting pages, escapes
the sun's terrifying beauty,
hurls itself down into darkness.

The Empty Notebook Meditates on a Fig Tree
  in the Baths at Baia

The world is full of things
longing for their stories.
A fig tree growing upside
down in a domed chamber,
ripe fruit falling on mosaic
floor. Seeds of figs watch
emperors still bathing in
green pools. Echoes of
murmur, slices of scream.
Nero's mother still directs
the soldier's sword to her
offending womb. History's
witness, marble and concrete
crumbling in the murderous air.

The Empty Notebook Looks at Diane Arbus

The empty notebook constructs loss
from what is missing
in the picture—the more
the picture tells, the less
the viewer knows. What parts
are fading? What ideas are
about to be forgotten?
What is tedious can be
sinister. What is familiar
can be made exotic.
The empty notebook regrets
the present isn't the past
and despairs of it ever
becoming the future.

The Empty Notebook Dreams About Jasper Johns

Gray

color of emptiness

color of fog

color of nothing

Possible light/possible darkness.

Gray water, gray window, gray flag.

Every dream leads to another:

a to b, 1 to 2.

like a man jumping from a ship

into the Gulf of Mexico,

his hands and his feet

leave their imprint on the deck.

Man going overboard—

arc of a body

swimming through air

flying through water.

This is the arc of his story.

The Empty Notebook at the Ballet

Puffy-shirted boys in tights bend low
and simper, try to keep empty tutus
floating in the air above them. The empty
notebook slumps in its seat, its pages flat
and sullen, outside the field of movement.
Tutus are tedious as feathers. The empty
notebook longs for anything to happen—
something real, tenderness, terror, something
surprising. And then the program changes,
different music, a heart-stopping leap, a turn that
changes pulse to music, music to pulse,
one dancer catches another, throws her into
oblivion, one intervenes when she is almost
lost, almost gone, but somehow lands on
shoulders—a dancer who wasn't even there
before. The empty notebook learns precision
and trust can twist the impossible into
something like safety, something real,
something like home. The empty notebook
climbs into the pocket of its seatmate,
planning future leaps and turns as
it travels to an unknown destination.

The Empty Notebook Sings Puccini

Che gelide paginine,
what frozen little pages—
the empty notebook sings,
then whispers its secret
name to the audience
coughing up pages of icy
notes on treble clefs that
march up and down
the staff they share empty
space with. Aging tenors
in patent leather shoes drink
wine in student cafés where
bohemians go to complain
of poverty and the uselessness
of life while high notes break
their hearts in unheated garrets
and die without reproach.
Meanwhile a famous singer
elopes with her artist boyfriend,
who is hiding a dissident
on the run. The soprano stabs
a smarmy baritone government
hotshot who has locked her in his
office with a fancy dinner and plans
for seduction while having her
boyfriend tortured in the basement.
The empty notebook identifies with
every role—coughs, sings, writhes
in pain then stabs itself with a pencil.

How the Empty Notebook is Carried

brown bag   lunch bag
feed bag   doggie bag
lawn bag   laundry bag
grab bag
            Baghdad
paper bag   diaper bag
tea bag   vacuum bag
dirt bag   scum bag
            sleeping bag
shopping bag   hand bag
eye bag   air bag
urine bag   trash bag
plasma bag   duffle bag
body bag

The Empty Notebook's Lost Memories

Before the shelf: a paper bag—the stick
and sheen of other notebooks? Or was it
Paris—an African tango palace, ebony
women pressed against yellow-suited men,
the heat of lunging bodies? Or was there
a dim bedroom in Washington Heights,
a man singing a thousand-year-old lullaby,
with no words, no hope? Maybe there was
a forest—waving shadows, drizzle, shriek
and murmur of wind, birdsong, scent
of moss, humus, pine sap. Yearly cycle:
bud/flower/leaf/drop. The sun's arc
beyond branches, moon's sweep in
tree-tops. Hum of life before the fall.

Advice from the Empty Notebook

Never be the empty notebook.
Never flutter on the line, lifeless
in a back lot like laundry, not like
a starling strangled in the branches.
Never be erasable, never blink,
never stare soulless out of bloodshot
sockets at grackles perching on
fence posts, cackling over the
muddy gutters. Don't sing about
not knowing, not seeing. Never
unlearn the whistling spark that
shreds the air to splatter the cosmos.
The point of saying vanishes.
It mistakes itself for vision, but
don't believe it for a minute. Pretend
a durable satisfaction. Pretend it will
not break. Pretend you do not fester;
are not pokeweed, or a pincushion.
Not intergalactic dust. Not a dying star.
Pretend you are not a black hole.

The Empty Notebook and Immortality

The empty notebook knows its only
talent is emptiness, but it wishes for
pages blue with writing while imagining
an afterlife: on file, recycled, scrapped,
in storage. It dreams reincarnation,
encyclopedia, checkbook, newspaper,
document, cinder flying out of the ashes.
The empty notebook looks for a signal
for everything to unravel—a point,
a line, a start to any story, an indication
of a phrase, a word, a letter—anywhere
speech leaves its droppings. It knows
how sound disappears between pages,
but the shape it has taken remains.

Notes

The original titles of the imitation poems, found on pages 30 - 44 of this manuscript, are as follows:

Amergin: *Song of Amergin* (Celtic, 9th century)
Celan: *Little Night*
Dante: *O You That Pass Along Love's Way*
Montale: *The Storm* (or *La Bufera*)
Lorca: *Dawn*
Li Po: *Alone and Drinking Under the Moon*
Darwish: *Words*
Ovid: *Metamorphoses*
Neruda: *Walking Around*
Popa: *Pig*
Virgil: *The Aenid* (first two stanzas)
Williams: *Nantucket*
Amichai: *Third Resurrection*

About the Author

Susan Thomas has published stories, poems and translations in many journals and anthologies. She has won the Iowa Poetry Award from Iowa Review, the Ann Stanford Prize from University of Southern California, first prize from the Spoon River Review and New York Stories and the 2010 MR Prize from the Mississippi Review. Red Hen Press published her collection, *State of Blessed Gluttony* (2004), which won their Benjamin Saltman Prize and *Last Voyage: Selected Poems of Giovanni Pascoli* (2010), which was co-translated with Deborah Brown and Richard Jackson. She also has two chapbooks, *The Hand Waves Goodbye* (Main Street Rag, 2002) and *Voice of the Empty Notebook* (Finishing Line Press, 2007).

Fomite
Burlington, Vermont

Fomite is a literary press whose authors and artists explore the human condition -- political, cultural, personal and historical -- in poetry and prose.

A fomite is a medium capable of transmitting infectious organisms from one individual to another.

Loisaida

by Dan Chodorokoff

Catherine, a young anarchist estranged from her parents and squatting in an abandoned building on New York's Lower East Side is fighting with her boyfriend and conflicted about her work on an underground newspaper. After learning of a developer's plans to demolish a community garden, Catherine builds an alliance with a group of Puerto Rican community activists. Together they confront the confluence of politics, money, and real estate that rule Manhattan. All the while she learns important lessons from her great-grandmother's life in the Yiddish anarchist movement that flourished on the Lower East Side at the turn of the century. In this coming of age story, family saga, and tale of urban politics, Dan Chodorkoff explores the "principle of hope", and examines how memory and imagination inform social change.

❧ ❧ ❧

When You Remember Deir Yassin

by R.L Green

When You Remember Deir Yassin is a collection of poems by R. L. Green, an American Jewish writer, on the subject of the occupation and destruction of Palestine. Green comments: "Outspoken Jewish critics of Israeli crimes against humanity have, strangely, been called "anti-Semitic" and as well as the hilariously illogical epithet "self-hating Jews." As a Jewish critic of the Israeli government, I have come to accept it these accusations as a stamp of approval and a badge of honor, signifying my own fealty to a central element of Jewish identity and ethics: one must be a lover of truth and a friend to the oppressed, and stand with the victims of tyranny, not with the tyrants, despite tribal loyalty or self-advancement. These poems were written as expressions of outrage, and of grief, and to encourage my sisters and brothers of every cultural or national grouping to speak out against injustice, to try to save Palestine, and in so doing, to reclaim for myself my own place as part of the Jewish people." The poems are offered in the original English with Arabic and Hebrew translations accompanying each poem.

❧ ❧ ❧

Fomite
Burlington, Vermont

The Co-Conspirator's Tale

by Ron Jacobs

There's a place where love and mistrust are never at peace; where duplicity and deceit are the universal currency. *The Co-Conspirator's Tale* takes place within this nebulous firmament. There are crimes committed by the police in the name of the law. Excess in the name of revolution. The combination leaves death in its wake and the survivors struggling to find justice in a San Francisco Bay Area noir by the author of the underground classic *The Way the Wind Blew:A History of the Weather Underground* and the novel *Short Order Frame Up*.

Kasper Planet: Comix and Tragix

by Peter Schumann

Kasper from Persian Ghendsh-Bar carrier of **treasures** What treasures Treasures of junk Degrader of the Pre**ciou**sness system Also from India Vidushaka Also medieval subversive thrown out **of** cathedral into marketplace A midget speaking swazzel language which **cops** don't speak

Views Cost Extra

by L.E. Smith

Views that inspire, that calm, or that terrify – all come at some cost to the viewer. In *Views Cost Extra* you will find a New Jersey high school preppy who wants to inhabit the "perfect" cowboy movie, a rural mailman disgusted with the residents of his town who wants to live with the penguins, an ailing screen writer who strikes a deal with Johnny Cash to reverse an old man's failures, an old man who ponders a young man's suicide attempt, a one-armed blind blues singer who wants to reunite with the car that took her arm on the assembly line -- and more. These stories suggest that we must pay something to live even ordinary lives.

Fomite
Burlington, Vermont

The Empty Notebook Interrogates Itself

by Susan Thomas

The Empty Notebook began its life as a literal metaphor for a few weeks of what Susan Thomas thought was writer's block, but was really the struggle of an eccentric persona to take over her working life. It won. For the next three years everything she wrote came to her in the voice of the Empty Notebook, who, as the notebook began to fill itself, became rather opinionated, changed gender, alternately acted as bully and victim, had bizarre adventures in exotic locales and developed a somewhat politically-incorrect attitude. It then began to steal the voices and forms of other poets and immortalized itself in various poetry reviews. It is now thrilled to collect itself in one volume.

My God, What Have We Done?

by Susan Weiss

a world afflicted with war, toxicity, and hunger, does what we do in our private lives really matter? Fifty years after the creation of the atomic bomb at Los Alamos, newlyweds Pauline and Clifford visit that once-secret city on their honeymoon, compelled by Pauline's fascination with Oppenheimer, the soulful scientist. The two stories emerging from this visit reverberate back and forth between the loneliness of a new mother at home in Boston and the isolation of an entire community dedicated to the development of the bomb. While Pauline struggles with unforeseen challenges of family life, Oppenheimer and his crew reckon with forces beyond all imagining.

Finally the years of frantic research on the bomb culminate in a stunning test explosion that echoes a rupture in the couple's marriage. Against the backdrop of a civilization that's out of control, Pauline begins to understand the complex, potentially explosive physics of personal relationships.

At once funny and dead serious, *My God, What Have We Done?* sifts through the ruins left by the bomb in search of a more worthy human achievement.

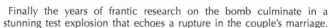

Fomite
Burlington, Vermont

Improvisational Arguments is written in free verse to capture the essence of modern problems and triumphs. The poems clearly relate short, frequently humorous and occasionally tragic, stories about travels to exotic and unusual places, fantastic realms, abnormal jobs, artistic innovations, political objections, and misadventures with love.

≋ ≋ ≋

"The activity of art is based on the capacity of people to be infected by the feelings of others." Tolstoy, *What is Art?*

Made in the USA
Charleston, SC
30 October 2011